Poetry Corners

2023

Bainbridge Island Press

Poetry

Tamarah Rockwood
Editor

Corners

2023

Bainbridge Island Press

Bainbridge Island, WA

Bainbridge Island
P R E S S

Poetry Corners is published annually. Learn more and make submissions to: https://www.poetrycorners.com/
Copyright © 2023

Published in 2023 by Bainbridge Island Press
Bainbridge Island, WA
https://bainbridgeislandpress.com

Printed in the United States of America

ISBN: 978-1-961451-02-5 (Second Edition, 2023)
ISSN: 2837-7508

Cover design: Ben Rockwood

9 8 7 6 5 4 3 2

Dedication

In memory of Bainbridge Island Treasure,
Nancy Rekow

Contents

Poetry Corners

2023

Bainbridge Island Press

Benediction

By Cindy Vandersluis

Rewind this life and patterns emerge like
gold in the miner's pan -- at first hidden, then gleaming and
beckoning with memories both sweet and bitter.

Someone once said,
"Déjà vu is just the brain
converting short-term memory to long."
But magic exists --
in the propitious telephone call,
in the touch that sets forth a lightening-like current,
in the vibration of color announcing the sunrise.

This is my rebirth,
when hope blows in from the ocean.

Although I'm tired, I take a walk
through the playground of my youth.
Cherry blossoms swirl overhead in a benediction.

The snowy owl
the angel
the red rose --

anything can be a prayer, an awakening
to this new season of our lives.

Rendition

By Kim Hamilton

Dark curls damped against his skull
as an infant crowning through waves

the elder's bones an easy float
thin veins and flesh a kind of raft

inside a raft. His young friend
guides his course, their voices

soar, *Fly Me to the Moon*,
fills the air and blots

the lifeguard's shout to walk
the swimmers splash and turn

at the wall. We turn to liquid joy
Let me see what life is like...

The pool's blue eye blinks breaking
the surface tension, the flail and song.

Longing, noun

By Carol Despeau Fawcett

1. to yearn for something or someone unattainable or distant, 2. a hole inside yourself, 3. the moment you realize those new earrings, or that new poetry book is not what you really need, 4. the last time he smiled at you and your words tumbled back down your throat like stones, 5. an unfinished love poem.

Poiesis

By Stephen Edwin Lundgren

My Father made the Boat that I own
That hull within which I yet travel
Domestic, crossing the bay to shop, to work
Industrious, out to the fjord entrance to fish
Adventures, into the gulf among rocks, islands
Recreational, on a quiet safe lake at sunset
We both have bentwood flat ribbing, boney chests
I breathe within its confines, working the oars
Seated on thwarts with wicker weaves
Fore, the small deck with ensign pole, my flag
Aft, the transom, hinged rudder, motor mount
(Mid, a mast step for a sail I have never dared raise)
Two adult bodies long, with a cutter's bow
Similar to the log canoes' displacements
From another coastline, chasing the same fish
Maybe my father did not really build this hull
Nevertheless, it is mine, that he gave to me
With his tool chests, for when I make my own
Poem about a boat.

Bainbridge Island Press

Memory Gone Astray

By Judy Rosen

Struggling fiercely to recall
what's been forgotten
luscious details become
blurred like campfire smoke
burning your eyes until
you move to the outer edge
and become an observer
of laughing conversing friends
whose names you no longer remember
in a happy scene you'll never forget

Bainbridge Forest Sonnet

By Rayne Lacko

The path ahead lies hidden by branches,
Fallen leaves, tiny paw prints, scuttled stones.
Rubber boots and woolen socks, panting dog,
Find buried passage revealing unknowns.

Lush forest footpaths, my trusted healers
Fungi, lichen and moss, tree-trunk abodes,
Four seasons' hearth, a home for wet creatures,
Rotifers, tardigrades, and nematodes.

Keen winds shake the leafage green and tender
Glistening dew pearls bespeckle, adorn
Fairy princess's woodland bedchamber.
Verdant archway of fern fronds, native-born.

Cross a running brook with a peaceful heart,
The woods are my comfort, sweet counterpart.

Bainbridge Island Press

Rain, Pacific Northwest

By Carol Despeaux Fawcett

It
slaps
and taps.
Drips and
drizzles. Pounds
my house, a tantrum-
my troll. It falls like lead
bullets from an overburdened
sky. Angles a way in, slants under
windowsills, drips into Tupperware.
Rivers down windows like torrents of
tears. It searches for something to hold it,
stop it, contain its cataclysm. It pelts the sun-
room roof like clamshells falling from the sky.
Outside my window, it hounds the holly tree, tears
red berries from leaves. It squalls through sailboat
masts, pummels my hummingbird feeder. It spits
down from heaven like a disgruntled god. It
soddens deck furniture, swamps gutters,
seeps past my barriers, and washes
me—pluviophile, lover
of rain—clean.

First Rain

By Robert Vandersluis

Seattleites are a funny bunch,
gleeful as children
in the first real rain of the season,
celebrating a waterproof fortitude unknown
to any but amphibians.
Walking to the ferry from my office,
the rain is coming down like my morning shower,
yet everyone **after you's** you, smiling,
cold, yet oddly happy, old skills returning.
Those born here retreat like
box turtles into their hooded jackets,
the uniform of the proud native.
Some even skip the hood,
ceasing to care about the resulting sodden hairstyle.
Those of us who've been here awhile,
but have yet to eschew the umbrella,
have learned to alternate between the
light grip of a child's hand to save strength
for that of a Roman gladiator round a short sword
for those random gusts of wind.
At home we'll regale our families, so to speak,
with how terrible it was on the commute,
committing the sin of pride.

Bainbridge Island Press

Ten Ways to Un-Island Yourself at an Eagle Harbor Bookstore Poetry Reading

By Kristi Helgeson

1. Tell your neighbor who did her thesis on Paul Valery thirty years ago about the reading and ask her to go with you.
2. Bring Prosecco and your Czech Grandmother's kolaches to share.
3. Offer to get refreshments for the Island Treasure sitting next to you.
4. During the Q&A, ask the poet which of their collections they like the most and, in the asking (but only if true), mention that all of their collections have moved and transformed you.
5. Also mention how much you loved the line about the lemon tree.
6. Jot the line about the lemon tree in your commonplace book and plan to share it with your writing group as a writing prompt.
7. After the Q&A, buy a book and ask the poet to sign it, addressed to "The Citizens of Bainbridge Island."
8. Give the signed book to the librarian, who is also at the reading (and whose poetry collection hasn't yet found a publisher), so she can add it to the library's poetry collection.
9. As the crown hovers around the poet after the reading, help the bookstore owner discreetly fold and stack the chairs before saying *Thank you and What a lovely reading.*
10. Back at home, before drifting off to sleep, tap out an email to the poet from your phone, thanking them for lines about lemon trees, small opportunities to un-island, and spreading light in the world.

Free

By Angela Borneman

In my home of weightlessness and still weather,
my singular heart is a cardinal,
warm and light in all seasons,
a scarlet bastion of liberty

green is the laughter at my hearth
the thump and blush of a pirouette
fills the kitchen
the loofah of a guitar riff
scrubs the air
a teary monstera - overly loved - pouts by the table

At night
a lone slipper sits dutifully at the side of my bed
the dog comes in, contrite and waggy
offering the other for ransom
I slip into a depression shaped by time and water
and my heels stutter against the cool sheets

I am perennial.
a prodigal daughter returned home
day after day, I wake to the mundane
and its never-ending magic

Bainbridge Island Press

Free of Fear

By Ruth Marcus

What do we stand on
when the sun's shadows
narrow our view
   are we angels of light
   or dragons roaring
   sleepless night after night

yes, dip into the pond
to relieve the heat
on the brink of doubt
comfort your mind, what is this about

what keeps us afloat
when we find ourselves
in a log jam, weeping
among downed friends—

still, we stand
in the face of fierce winds
bobbing in tears, life sustaining
free of our fears

Unfurling

By Tamera Roza

Without knowing
I've been holding

A fury of pain
Inside my hands

I yield to yearning
They are now unfurling

Imperfect heart doing
The best I can

I rest my fists
In firsts, take risks

Stay still, where
Once I ran

I'm standing, falling
Open palm calling

Please hold me
If you can

Bainbridge Island Press

The Canopy in My Daughter's Room

By Anne Laird

I promised her many things, including a tattoo,
if only she would do one more round of chemo.
Instead she wanted a queen bed, with canopy,
for the months she had left.

It arrived sooner than I wanted,
and when we attached the canopy
it flowed like a bridal train on a June breeze.
When it dangled behind her giant Make-a-Wish TV,
her bed became her private theatre.

There she entertained friends who brought snuggles
and raucous laughter, tears and news from school.
She insisted on candles for the table footing her bed,
so I tied back the fabric.
Her two puppies jumped and chewed the corners.

Our favorite moon, a crescent, waned in late autumn skies,
while inside her silent billowing cave,
I smoothed the hair just starting to grow on her head.

Gratitude to Nancy Rekow for her inspirational poem
The Ocean in my Brother's Room-- for Doren

Candy

By Amanda Williamsen

Don't go in the river. All the time,
they told us that. Don't go across the road,
or in the woods, or down in the ravine
where somebody's old stove lay rusted red.
That's tetanus, they said. Don't stomp the beans.
It hurts the yield. Don't stuff the outhouse full
of sticks. No matches, knives, or kerosene.
No saw. No nail gun, dammit. What the hell
is wrong with you? Can't leave you kids alone.
Don't use the boat. Don't put mosquito spray
cans in the fire. Blows up, dumbass. And don't
go in those abandoned cabins. We said okay.
Ah, childhood. Gnawing gutters, window panes.
Waiting for a witch who never came.

published 2016, Red Wheelbarrow, Vol. 17

Soon Enough

By Teia McCoskery

Summer can't come soon enough
I need sun on my skin
Salt in my hair
Grass under my feet

Summer can't come soon enough
I need 70's music and Yacht Rock all day
Music blaring in my head
As I walk down the street
Record player skips in "The Jackson's"

Summer can't come soon enough
I'm sick of the cold and sick of being sick
I need shivers from the sea water
Not from colds

Summer can't come soon enough
I need to be out there
Free
In the sun
Just as I am in the summer
The real
True me.

Girl in Red Tennies

By Joy Sprague

Toes push off patch in fresh mown green grass
So red tennies can fly up to blue sky
Nurturing hands press firm at her back
Lifting her higher toward evergreen limbs
As red tennies fly touching blue sky
Small hands fist-clench rough rope at her sides
And branch above creaks from butt on wood seat
While red tennies pump…up, and up, and up
Songbirds sing, animal clouds fluff and fade to blue
Faster, faster, faster she shouts, "underdog pleeeease"
She dips back down to tummy dropping gut-giggles
Where her red tennies fly up to blue sky

Bainbridge Island Press

Pink Chrysanthemum

By Stefani Galaday

Still she stood in the vase
upright and straight as if no
thing no one could sway her
the other floral mates drooped
as if sleep had overtaken them
bent down under gravity's weight
but you there without a tinge of wink
or nod I cannot help but take strength
from your example to live transplanted
to be cut off from your native soil without
roots or culture
trumpeting alone
unsullied.

Novice

By Anne Kundtz

Bikes rest lifeless on tan lawns
curtains closed   doors shut
swamp coolers murmur
sun is just beyond noon

at the bottom of the street
the abandoned orchard
forgets to   breathe

I duck beneath branch whips
where cracked apples cling
sit cross-legged on leaf duff
close my eyes

try to hear beyond the quiet:

bees step across dried apple ooze
ants shuffle in solemn lines
crisp leaves shift over field mice
burrowing behind me.

I apprentice myself
to this mystery
ask to be let in.

Out on the street heatwaves hum
their single note on asphalt
the tanned mountain is silent
in the relentless blue sky.

Bainbridge Island Press

Childhood

By Linda B. Myers

We flew! Hair streaming no helmets to hold it back
galloping through harvested fields, soft stalks
slapping Nugget and Rebel in their cinched bellies.

Barn cat scratches, rusty nail scrapes,
hay poking at our eyes as we tunneled wormholes
between the high stacked bales.
We tiptoed on rotting beams high over the sty
death by hog below.

We won the West and WWII, cap guns smoking hot
skating biking and dodging beanballs,
no safety gear or stranger fear.
We traveled as far as our legs would take us
till Aunt Mary's big bell called us home.

No pre-arranged play dates. No adult supervision.
We weren't safe. But we were free.

We are here.

By Vanee Lyon

We are here.
Beneath the blue of a passing sky
Beneath the warmth of a tilting sun
I lay here. Enraptured by the complexity of being
Who am I?
I gaze at the sun once more. What is this?
I sit, and stare across the horizon. I walk slowly along the shore, sand in-between my toes
The waves slowly crash against my feet washing the sand away each time
The wind caresses my face, the breeze is warm.
I breathe deeply. Who am I ? What is this?
The wind loudly blows against my ear whipping my hair in all directions.
It's says sweetly - this is life, you are life.
You are each speck of sand beneath your feet
Each shell that's laid upon this beach
Each bird that soars above the sky
Each tear that falls from your eye
You are each flower that blooms in a tree
You are you and you are me
You are everything good, bad, scary, and bright
You are the reflection of the universe's light
You are you, and I am me
Together, we are we.

Bainbridge Island Press

Hummingbirds Don't Smile

By Robert Vandersluis

At least that is what my wife says,
making what she supposes is a hummingbird face,
so serious. So very serious. That's what happens
when you rarely rest your wings, she explains,
when you keep flapping while everyone else
kicks it on a convenient wire or tree limb.
She has thought about this.
Hummingbirds take life seriously, she says.
I mean they have to be in constant pursuit of calories
just like those lean and mean people we
meet in life, the ones who ask you for your fries
having demolished their own.
But here's the thing. If you have ever seen an
unfurled hummingbird tongue--
seemingly twice the length of his little head—
how could he not have a sense of humor?
I suppose the only possible reason
is that the head space normally reserved for happiness
is filled with the organ he needs to suck up nectar.
I never wish a reincarnation so cruel as to make me
an unhappy hummingbird in search of carnations.
I reassure her that no loving God would ever
reincarnate her into an unhappy hummingbird,
and we finish our cognac on that happy note.

The Waterfront Chickens

By Tamarah Rockwood

They were like children wandering hungry,
Away from their green home and then scratching
With clawed toes the ground of Town & Country

Bobbing their heads for bugs, for seeds, pecking
The parking lot as if the world was clear
To them, the buff birds with full-feathered wing

Whose paths passed beneath the pines, the cedars,
The parked cars, shopping carts, the dancing feet
As if they were the island troubadour

Chanting gentle melodies of incomplete,
Brief love affairs they have had with roosters
Of times gone by – memories bittersweet

Like young leaves plucked too early by the street,
Like fading memories that rest, a beat.

Bainbridge Island Press

My Hen Fanny

By Judy Duncan

Fanny hen throat-hums
to her baby chicks
like a cat purring
in your lap

she eats baby mice
pecks a small garter
snake & swallows
in gasping gulps

her right eye spies a slug
left, a circling hawk
yet she cannot view
directly in front of her beak

Fanny loves to roll
like a buffalo
in a dust bowl
under the lilac bush

Birdcage

By Sharon Armstrong Ostenson

I once bought a bird cage
Not one to hold feathered beauties
It holds a candle now, door wide open
A reminder that I am free
Free of my caged thoughts
Worries, resentments, past darkness
My bird circles back, wanting to return and
Close the door, safe to remain
Angry, afraid, resentful
I imagine again the door opening
My freedom returns if for just a moment
This morning I carry my cuppa out
Onto a sunlit deck and hear
the chatter of birds at the feeder
Under the Blue Spruce
Squirrels too have come for the feast
Free to cavort with one another

Scampering off with their prize
I have not noticed lately my bird cage
Door open, hanging under the porch eve
I notice it today and remember to fly

Bainbridge Island Press

Adoration of the Wings

By Kim Hamilton

He says use tweezers, as her fingers braille

the air catchers. She strokes

    their sleepy furrows where the codes reside

  a sweater cuff to ravel
the drift of eggs to hatch their way out
chewing vacancies in the shapes of stars.

  Nearly weightless now, their bodies quilt
the porch light globe, scrim the light

  each one a book of common days, exit lines
scrolled across their wings.

    She pours the still bodies to her white cloth
the rain of copper heads and thoraxes, wing bits iridescing
palest green, gossamer sari rippled and flung-

    What a mess, he says at the feeler quirked
  like half a thought, turned back, the body she can't identify,
a blade of sedge. Arms herringboned across its chest.

Adore the gorgeous corpse, she breathes then types

their flub and bother, the tattoo they beat to panes

      dividing each from light, the cosmic smack.

May we glitter in our going, is what she says.

I Went Out to Hear

By Lisa Ashley

birdsong. Layered
in springblue air like cream icing
slipped into cake sweet
joy praise to life
the bees' didgeridoo humming
me forward I found a yellow honeybee
dancing in the arms of ivory pistils lavender
petals six times its size waved
beneath like a geisha's fan
in the teahouse breeze.
The bee brings me to drala
time-transcendent enchantment
standing stock still
eyes locked my knees grow heavy
with pollen I beat
my fevered wings lift off
in this singular moment wish
my way on to the next flower.

Bainbridge Island Press

Welcome the Pelicans

By Carl Jensen

I see them flying
A line of dark sparks
Teasing the neck of a wave
Winging not in unison
Strung out like one long train.

I watch dazzled as they circle to land
A child's crown of colored pencils
Made of glass radiating light splendors
Flight splendor.

I wonder how one is made
Clay, while it's still soft
Roll a cylinder, scratch grooves
Pinch a crook and fashion openings
This crazy saxophone of a bird!

The Gardeners

By Judy Rosen

In March hundreds of humans
emerge from their winter dormancy.
Like butterflies they arrive quietly
without announcement.

Knees on ground.
Head down.
Hands in dirt.
Properly positioned
for
removing weeds,
planting seeds,
spreading compost,
to
grow vegetables,
nurture colorful plants,
beautify their yards One Inch at a time.

By November their backs hurt,
their fingers are stiff, their knees ache.
They gratefully sink into winter's depth
putting physical labor aside until
March beckons them to the garden.

Bainbridge Island Press

Slugs

By John Davis

Slow slimeballs
  thick and sticky-trail warriors
    mucus marauders
harvest the garden of mimulus
  daisies dahlias
    antennae raised like rabbit ears
of a television set
  leave a silver trail
    that glows in moonlight
like fluorescent stripes
  we wore on shoulders
    under black lights
when we'd dance
  slow dances
    maladjust our selves
into their selves
  warm our warmth
    against their warmth
leave an invisible trail
  of love if that's what it was
    when the music stopped.

The Myth of Adorina

By Steve Parmelee

Once upon a fabled time
She wanders lost, say books of rhyme
Adorina's never done
Plucking petals one by one
    he loves me, he loves me not, he loves me, he loves me not

Prescient petals, sweet cologne
Drop wilted now to cobblestone
Pied pink prayers will dot her trail
To stave off fears; to no avail
    he loves me, he loves me not, he loves me, or so she thought

From daffodil spring wakeup call
To marigold late blooming fall
Flowers realize fleeting glory
Blossom's blaze is transitory
    he loves me, he loves me not, he loves me, my heart he's got

Desecrating Frost's cliché
Nothing pink can ever stay
Hardest hue to hold she'd say:
To love with grace, again, today

Bulldozer

By Steve Parmelee

In the sand between woodsheds,
under the splintered rope swing seat,
half-buried among other toy trucks is a bulldozer
that may have once been yellow and red.

The rusted blade frozen downward,
it just pushes away.
Yet that's what she's built for, not to carry or lift
like the trusty tilt dump trucks and loaders.
She just pushes away, scarring ruts, dredging dirt.

There's a draw to the damaged, and an impulse to fix,
fingers fiddling with the tall hand-crank crane truck,
winding found string up stripped pulley gears.
But with the rubber treads of the dozer long gone,
she's stuck, immobile unless shoved.

Her pitted steel surface sun and salt faded,
so well-built, but battered and dinged.
Handled and thrown by countless wild boys,
tell-tale signs of their roughness, of course
but showing nothing of their tenderness, no.
That would not leave a trace.

Skunk

By Jeremy Moff

Standing on the sidewalk waiting for a Uber, in amazement at how many new high rises have sprung up... Cold wind and slight northwest mist...

I did not see him, not until his hand slid across my back shoulders, electrical current a flash, there he was directly in front of me, not the grown man with the awkward gate, hands bent inward, fingers twisted, repeatedly saying, skunk, skunk... no this was him... much younger on the beach playing in the sand. He and another little boy are building a sand castle... laughing and running... a little peace of heaven. A black puppy with a white tail... licking faces.... More giggles... a little girl asks, can I pet your puppy?". The boy says, "sure can; watch out, he likes to give kisses." What is his name.... Skunk... Skunk... Skunk...

The force of his torso catching me off balance almost knocks me into traffic... I regain my footing and turn to see this disheveled mid-twenties man... arms moving out of sync... curled hands, twisted fingers... side-stepping... circling me, looking at the ground... though seeing beyond... searchingly calling out "skunk, skunk, Skunk..." pirouettes forward and falls back... side stepping into the Seattle mist...

I'm Addicted

By Teia McCoskery

Your delicate wrapping and
Unwrapping
Around my fingers
I run my fingers down your back
Marveling at your beauty

I think of you everywhere
Picking at my skin in place of you
Imagining everything beautiful
We can make

God I love you
Beautiful colors and textures

Ugh I love it
I love you crochet

At the Rim

By Emily Jane Mockett

The rim of the coffee cup
Matters to me, the most
The smooth texture of warm baked earth
That once was gently held
Between the potter's bare hands
Shaped with a loving purpose
Where my lips now kiss the liquid good morning
Greeting the day in silence
Where my nose gathers the scents of my ritual
Flushing me with anticipatory joy
Where my eyes stare into the middle distance
Marinating me in the sauce
Made of last night's dreams & today's possibilities
Where my fingers wrap around the top of the sacred vessel
Like how I took communion as a child—
Carefully cupped to where my thumbs & fingertips touch
Here in the morning at the rim of my coffee cup
I kneel before the Universe
Gratefully in awe of the lip of this new day
To begin again—
Awake, alive, alert to the sensation
I am already kissed by Life

Bainbridge Island Press

Geezer Gear

By David Stallings

When we come to a bend in the trail
we take one of our frequent breaks.
Randy announces it's time for the contest
he cooked up—a free brownie for the oldest
but still working hiking tackle.

Bruce wears his ancient red hunting shirt.
The green gaiters Jim wears are 30 years old,
Bill sports an original North Face rain shell,
and Randy, wool pants once worn in the army.
But my 1955 Boy Scout pocket knife,
passed around the circle, wins the prize.

I open its sharp blade
to divide the prize,
but then Randy brings out
extra brownies for all.

Ode to My Tall Tree Friend

By Ruth Marcus

I lean against you as you sway—
arms wrapped around your wet bark,
sweet scent of rain,
you and I holding on—
stand in the dark of night and light of day.

How many arms have hugged you?
How many feathered friends visit—
tweeting, screeching, caroling?
Offering a branch to rest and build a nest—
an ellipsis between egg...birth...first flight.

You, mighty friend, withstand fierce winds.
Lean, bend and bow as if teaching Tai Chi—
the art of grace and balance.
Yes, like you, I moan and know I'm not alone—
I too, will eventually fall.

You whisper, whoosh and creak
but never complain—teaching me
the art of standing through wind
and stormy weather
together, until our time has come.

The Prettiest Tree

By Dianne Knox

Is there a prettier tree than the Madrona?
Oh, you may think so, with your canopied elms
covering the streets on a hot summer night, an
evening stroll turned processional at twilight

Or, maybe you think maples with palm-stretched
leaves as big as watermelons to cantaloupe are it.
But, the Madrona has complexity in color, texture,
wandering limbs, waxy leaves that attach

to your eye, flutter and fall thick on the ground
cushioning your gait, gathering around footsteps
then pushed away into muffled mounds awaiting
the next passers-by keen eye.

Madrona's peeling bark – green giraffe, to red silky
reveals inner feels, layered personality, almost human.

North Star

By Ray Monde

On a rare clear night, I look up
Into the darkness
To pinpricks of light that are alien
Like me
A foreigner in a northern land
And I am betrayed
Looking for solace
In the once familiar night sky
And I think if I die here
My bones will be restless
In the cold mossy earth
My hollow sockets
Staring into the dark sky
Dreaming of warm nights
And echoes of cicadas screaming

Bainbridge Island Press

Country Music

By Teia McCoskery

God I hate it
twang & beer & boys
blasting out of sad
middle-aged men's windows
blaring past
in their old Ford F-250s

Then it started getting stuck
in my head
the words sounded poetic
& the rhymes about beer didn't
bother me as much

The guitar was nice &
I started to learn it
My Avril Lavigne turned to Tim McGraw
My MCR turned to Zach Bryan

God I hated it
Stupid Country music

Buttons

By Sharon Armstrong Ostenson

Buttons appear unexpectedly
Seemingly out of nowhere
Out of place
Gaudy, useless
Buttons thought long lost
Pop back on like shiny confetti
Far too bright
As soon as they appear
They fade and are gone again
Until the next button is pushed
Emotional buttons sewn on a cloak I keep taking off

Bainbridge Island Press

Things Unseen

By Marsha Cutting

There's a path—a shortcut to downtown—
that ends in a flight of stairs.

"They're going to take the stairs out," people say,
glancing at my wheelchair.
"Then you'll be able to use it."

"But what about the curb at our end?" I ask.

"Curb? There's no curb there."
"Pretty sure there is," I say.
They firmly deny its existence—so firmly that I go check.
Sure enough, it's there.

My neighbors mean me no ill--
they built me a raised garden bed, after all--
but curbs have no importance in their lives.
That which has no relevance remains invisible.

I think of this as I watch people with white skins
explain to my dark-skinned friend

what is—and isn't—racism.

Paper Planes

By John Weins
For Ezrah

The appropriations bill
fell dead in committee.
Still, without funding
my grandson has cobbled
together an air force worthy
of a banana republic–
no two planes exactly the same,
me at the Area 51 of the dining room table
heavy into research and development,
folding back delta wings,
smoothing leading edges,
adjusting ailerons
while he launches plane after plane
off the landing of the stairway.
Some fight imaginary MiGs,
banking and diving,
others circle slowly
conducting high-altitude surveillance,
while the crazy general of our
cat sits in the corner,
tail moving like a metronome–
ready to use his launch codes
if anything invades his airspace.

Bainbridge Island Press

Mask

By Tamera Roza

Hours, days, and minutes
I have pressed near and against your lips
Tasted the every of your tasting

I never tire of your in and out
The proof and wonder of your life
The closer I am to your sounds and wetness
The more useful and important I become

Just to be near you incites a flurry of needing
Without your strong hands
Holding and positioning me - just so
I am blank as plain paper

Ahh...But when you grab me
Thrust me to your mouth
Inhale my fibers and
Flaunt me like like the latest fashion
I am remarkable

Let me open doors for you
Let me be your all access pass to pleasure
Let me protect you

Failure

By Hanh Chau

Failure builds strength in me
with a lesson of perseverance
to remain strong in every situation
that comes into life with obstacles
despite the struggle, I endured
But I never surrender
and feel undaunted by defeat
I am tougher to know
to carry myself back up
with persistent
embrace as a learning experience
not to let it define me
to champion the cause
bring in the impossible
accomplish the goal
    I
      still
        stand
          strong

Bainbridge Island Press

Candlelight

By Jenny Coates

Never take a person's light
for granted.
Its flicker is a fragile thing,
to be savored as special, always
with reverence
for its evanescence.
You never know when
someone you love will exit
your life to cross
a threshold whose door is not
yet open to you.
Call them
now.
Hug them now.
Hold them dear, now.

Wabi Sabi

By Stefani Galaday

I live in a house made of wood
a box of a sort with two windows.
The biggest slides open to a porch
with a fence and a view of madrones
and oak. Inside a bed a tub and a kitchen
and shelves with books and fabric and paint.
Sometimes I leave to walk with a friend
to visit a shop or chat with a stranger
whose face I haven't met yet.
Enchanted, yes, this life that I have.
To the east two sons and their mates.
To the west a daughter and hers.
Last night I saw their father
on the zoom screen and
wept to see him anew.
His is-ness there enjoying
the moment with others.
At times life seems so broken and then
it gathers itself up and with a golden paste
it comes together again. Maybe the great
flood was composed of human tears
that split that morning's light
like a prism into a rainbow.

Bainbridge Island Press

Trapped in a Trapezoid

By John Davis

So bold those angles, those angels, those arcs
    and altitudes congruent on a page. How to be
        as equiangular as the diameter of this circle
    to that circle. Obtuse I could do. Never a polygon
never a prism with parallel faces. My protractors

unevened parallelograms. Radius and ratio rounded
    like rays in my head. What color the rectangle?
        What sound the cosine? What smell the secant,
    the taste of triangles, the touch of transversals?
Trapped in a trapezoid was more accurate. No change

in my brain in feel, form or shape.
    I dangled like the tangent of bone and marrow,
        touched a curve at only one point but that point
    was the closed surface I could live within
and I became the product of my own root.

It is there in the words

By Vanee Lyon

It is there in the words so delicately placed on the pages of books where we find our pain, our identity, our healing; beginning to unravel, to untangle. Until it is before us, line for line, word for
word. Then suddenly we see ourselves clearly as if we are standing before a freshly polished mirror.

How words placed so articulately on a page can paint a picture we've never seen with our eyes but have surely felt in our hearts.

How words can free us from pain we've long felt imprisoned by. Pain we've tried to escape from but couldn't.

How words can connect strangers, can bond them through the shared experience that is life.

Words have power, whether spoken or read. We find ourselves on the pages of books jumping from word to word, searching for something that we believe evades the capacity of the human
language. Until, it is there, laid delicately before us.

But often the words we search for, but fail to find, are born in the mouths of those we share this Earth with.

It is in that understanding that we become human.

We become human when
we speak with light and light only.

We become human when we speak without indulging the ego, when the words that we allow to escape from our lips carry with them the lambency that is love.

We become human when our words consider, when our words reinforce, when our words heed the pain of the beautiful array of people who walk this planet.

We do not find ourselves in speaking for - ourselves. We find ourselves in speaking for others.

It is there before the mirror we stand, that once more our words allow us to wipe away the mire

This time not to see ourselves, but to see each other.

Bainbridge Island Press

Words

By Rex Olsen

Who knows which words will be preferred
Which ones employed and which, deferred

It isn't always conscious thought
It sometimes is, but often not

The words come bubbling, boiling out
As if they wanted, all, to shout

And then arrange themselves in line
My thoughts to order and define

The order is much clearer when
The words are written by my pen.

right here, just there

By Bobbie Morgan

the small white feather in the gutter
the shades of green in the lichen
the sudden swoop of eagle wings right in front of the house
the taste of chocolate in my mouth
the deep purple of dried rose petals on the kitchen counter
the warmth of bathwater as I slowly step in
the scent of minced garlic sautéing in the cast iron pan
the orange light flickering from the fireplace
the softness of the alpaca wool sweater against my arms
the intricacy of that fragile spider web dangling at the window
the beat of the Irish drum resonating through the radio
the silver reflection of the sky in the puddle at my feet

sometimes I just stop
and allow little moments in
through the envelope of threats that are wrapped around us
and when I stop for simple beauty, right here, just there,
I exhale amazement and keep going

Bainbridge Island Press

One Morning in May

By Sue Hylen

blue jays
whirl
through
thrum
drumming
rains
watering
my garden

swallows
soar
under
thunder
clouds
lightning
crackling
skies

clapping
with
a chorus
of
crows

Time Out

By Linda B. Myers

Time is a vanishing resource
like glacial ice
and old growth
and monarch butterflies
and I don't want to dwell on
lost time or wasted time or time sucks
when I have so little of it
left to fritter away.

Time is my enemy.
I won't waste pretty words
on such a slouching beast
when brief bouts of joy
take me next to no time at all.

Bainbridge Island Press

Slow to Rise

By Rayne Lacko

Darkness, stars
Too early
Cat meows
Stretch, yawn
Cold toes
on floor

Sleepy moon
Stubble kiss
Morning lips
Coffee grind
Steam, pour
Wake up

Wagging dog
Grumbling child
Pajama hug
Cereal rattles
in bowl
Sunrise breaks.

Tender Morning

By Jenny Coates

The world is hard.
Hold yourself tenderly
and find soft edges even
where it seems there are none.
Step slow out of bed into
the frosty sun
with your steaming tea.
Greet your dog's warm breath,
wet nose and silken ears
as all that matter.
Glance up and see what
the clouds are doing.
Sit still with a mind empty
of traffic for as
long as you
can. Then notice what
beckons.

Bainbridge Island Press

Lost Civilization

By John Weins

School's been canceled
and by eleven a.m. the snowmen
are full of themselves.
Leavened by heaven,
rolled in the dough of winter,
a recipe of low pressure and moist air,
they appear suddenly
in the strata of family albums,
beside smiling children
in snow pants and stocking caps-
these mad scientists of the front yard
shaping and sculpting
with the scalpels of their mittens
their newfound friends.

Doughboy bodies,
limbs made of limbs,
their crooked smiles
an orthodontist's dream.
Tomorrow the sun
will put them on a diet
and send them away.

Learning Trust

By Anne Kundtz

My son opens his door and I step back
from the porch and onto the grass.

Sadie, a blue heeler, rushes to my feet
to crouch and pee.
Jasper, a shepherd, races beyond me first,
then looks back, surprised he overshot,
hurries back to let me rough his fur.
They will welcome me every time this way, I know

As if I was the BEST person.
As if I could do no wrong.
As if I held all the love.
This is how it is to trust.

My fists unclench and the rope
to my heart sits slack in my hands.

Didn't You Know

By Karen Hall Gosson
Dedicated to Adam D.

How did it feel standing above the world
The day the world stood still for you

Didn't you know someone would miss you
Every soul you knew, including mine
How empty it is here without you
How were we to know we were out of time

How did the wind feel in your hair
As you took a moment standing there
Seeing the last sun rise in the east
Then you took your step to peace

Didn't you know someone would miss you
Every soul you knew, including mine
It's so empty here without you
Without your laugh, your smile, your life

What I wouldn't give to hold your hand
Tell you everything I didn't say
Anything to hold you back
Anything to make you stay

How did it feel standing above the world
The day the world stood still for you

Improvised

By Scot Hedrick

You didn't look
Because you feared the scene.
You didn't listen
Because you feared the music.
You didn't talk
Because you feared the script.
You preferred tableau to performance;
You preferred homily to honesty;
You preferred façade to authenticity.

So I was left alone to craft my story,
Following my truth,
Listening only to inspiration.

I could not be a figurine on your window sill;
I could not be a silver candelabrum polished free of blemish;
I could not be a television character from the black and white Fifties.
I could only be a single "me."
Unique.
Improvised.

Bainbridge Island Press

Dog and Squirrel

By Judy Drechsler

Ears laid back.
Rigid legs shiver with rage.
Mad whines split the air.
Nose pressed against glass.

Twitching nose.
Swishing brown tail.
Feet clutch top of wood fence
ready to sprint.

Door opens. Dog leaps out.
With wild barking
claws at fence, runs back and forth.

Squirrel streaks along fence top.
Leaps into the gnarled pear tree,
Darts to the giant red cedar,
disappears into leafy hideaway

Dog whines, settles in to wait.
Forever patient,
squirrel chatters his displeasure...
or maybe he's laughing.

Your Daily Poem online 2020

The Streets

By Mark Themann

The Streets in Buffalo cry out we are gritty
customers at the bar order beer and buffalo wings

The Streets of Seattle say we are sophisticated
as customers of Fran's Chocolates
buy fudge and patrons of the Seattle Art Museum
look at the European art collection

The Streets of Prague say Saint Wenceslas
and Jan Huss have walked on us
the music of Mozart is played at the Clementium

The streets of the National Theatre filled with patrons
who see Don Giovanni tormented in Hell

The Streets of Rome say we are the eternal city
Saint Paul and Saint Peter are buried beneath us
Michelangelo painted the Last Judgement
in the Sistine Chapel

Bainbridge Island Press

Banquet at The Manor House at Pleasant Beach after Tu Fu

By Kristi Helgeson

Through the checkered forest light
the strings of the lute
sing songs of the sea;
moist, flowing, waning.

The moon is crowned in constellations.
Swords burn sharp as darkness thatches
a roof over your flower path.

To be on a boat with you,
to think of the wine, the candles, the poetry contest
and the way the little brook
goes past the windy wits of the world.

Pioneer Square: Everywhere

By Nancy Fowler

A young man leans against the brick wall,

energy coiled, ready to spring,
like a boxer waiting
to dodge the next blow,
or to dance in close for a hit.

His feet tap, tap, tap,
in black leather boots
with glinting steel buckles,
bought by working odd jobs that he hated.

Bare chest thrust forward,
his silence cries I am a man!
daring the world to take him on,
daring himself to take on the world.

Battered ears and rough brown nipples,
pierced by dangling hoops and chains,
scoff at my old soft flesh.

Bainbridge Island Press

Blue Highways

By Judy Drechsler

Spider lines across the map,
freedom from routine and chores of home.
Meandering down the back roads,
no destination in mind

Wind in my face, suntanned arm
out the window.
One hand on the wheel.
Each bend in the road brings small slices of life

A farmer tills the field,
sheets flap in the wind.
A woman reaches
for more clothespins

She glances up
I pass through with a wave
and a nod
to strangers I will never see again.

Your Daily Poem online 2019 Ars Poetica art by Merle Jones 2015

Celebrity Commute

By Rebecca Christensen

Driving along the 3 towards Poulsbo
the trees lean across the highway
like fans along a runway,
my celebrity status in glory today
just for this one snowy day on my daily commute.

The trees sway in the wind
clapping boughs at my presence
causing icy crystals to rain down like glitter
surrounding my car in a
bejeweled gown of sunlit tulle.

Signs appear roped off/held back by snowbanks.
They click and pop by so fast
like paparazzi out for the frenzy.
I ignore them
unable to see their whole identity behind the
filmy sheen of icy lenses
hiding their true intent.

On this one day
on this one snowy, icy glorious morning
I achieve stardom.

Bainbridge Island Press

Shoreline

By Dianne Knox

Day is sinking into glorious.
From the dock planks, light settles.
Shadows fall into sky.

Calm is cast over dreamy scenery.
Shore green reeds reach into blue water.
Ripples float in sunset.

Lonely boat rests
after delivering human cargo
safely to port.

Our Springer listens
to evening frog and insect chatter while
guarding and protecting his space, his home.

Safe, still, relaxing, fine
Stuff of dreams
Smell of pine.

Looking out my window, Port Townsend

By Nancy Fowler

At this moment, there are no deer
on the grass, no crows or robins
on branches of the leaf bare maple.

They are snuggled somewhere safe
from today's pounding rain, as I am
in my study, book in my lap.

Tim is pushing a stroller up Blaine Street,
very bundled against the weather, only
his gait gives him away. It must be little
Milo in the carriage, not so little much longer.

The blue and white lights on at Deborah's house
cut through the daylight gloom. We both
put up lights on the same day, for the same
reason- a longing for cheerfulness.

What do you call something that isn't a wind chime
but hangs from the porch beam and twists
in the wind? Two long lines of metal, one blue,
one green, edged by small leaves. A double helix.

As I watch them turn, then reverse, over and over,
they remind me that despite the twists and turns
of the wind, all comes back to its center.

Bainbridge Island Press

Surely I Can

By David Stallings

quick free beer! (Birding mnemonic, olive-sided flycatcher)

To pedal back up
this long, steep hill
calls for a tuned mind.
Here, in the spring,
a favorite bird calls from a treetop
to assert his claim to this part
of the mixed forest along the road.
If he can fly here from South America
I can surely make it up this hill.
Even in winter I whistle his call
as I pedal up the hill.
His numbers in decline,
last year he made no appearance.
But I whistled on
as I do this spring morning.
At first I don't believe my ears,
but there, and there again.
This evening I toast his arrival
and the world we share.

The Amazon Burns

By Nancy Taylor

The Amazon burns—it's not in our news
though ten million species call it home.
What about the Howler monkeys' views?

This canopied lung our planet will lose
when we destroy rainforest's biome.
The Amazon burns—it's not in our news.

Impunity sparks land grabber abuse,
who deforest then burn logs for ashen loam.
What about jaguars' and pumas' views?

Jungles are converted into grassland hues,
logging and mining tear plant rhizomes.
The Amazon burns—it's not in our news.

Pleas for beef and leather light this fuse,
farmers profit more where cattle roam.
What about the Yanomami's views?

Demise of carbon-sinking trees incurs dues
returns it back to gas, depletes ozone.
The Amazon burns—it's not in our news.
What about the next generation's views?

Published in The Literary Nest, 2020

Bainbridge Island Press

The Potting Bench

By Rex Olsen

She'd asked for a potting bench for forty years, but then she left the garden.
So he built one, my grandfather. Rough-hewn, the bench and he.
Leaned a little, rocked. Unsteady, both of them.
Distressed. He was often distressed.
And come to think of it,
Potted.

Excisional Biopsy

By Amanda Williamsen

The night before the surgery, I lie down
beside my sleeping mother. In the dark
room, the bed is a raft undulating
with her breath. I want to cover myself
in water. In my own dark, in the flesh
of my breast, two tumors
roll like stones. I have carried them
for a year. Tomorrow, my first
birth will be bad fruit, abortive tangles
of fibers. I imagine my body unmoving
under other's hands. When we come home,
my mother will peel back the dressing
to show me the red, later white,
line of loss. Her chest rises evenly.
I am drifting through the night, one hand
over the small moons of my heart.

Baltimore Review, 2002

Bainbridge Island Press

Hard to Lee!

By Sue Hylen

Dad shouts
shoving
the Mary K's
thick wooden tiller
through
huff-blustering winds
over
Puget Sound's swirling waves.

His hazel eyes
beam
through
my hazel eyes
our
sandy brown hair
blowing wild
our
backs & butts
stretch over starboard
white waters
gushing
through
shadows & light.

Because

By Kirsten Lauer

Because they grew in
The darkness of shade
It was necessary
To reach ever higher
To kiss the light;
And then
Those roses
Bloomed
So much later than their peers
That their soft
Brightness
Persisted stubbornly
Well past the silent absence
Of colorful jays
Moved on
For winter.

Bainbridge Island Press

Spades and Hearts

By Diane Moser

I see her in the kitchen
cutting bread shapes
with cookie cutters
shaped like card suits: clubs,
diamonds, spades and hearts.

Her bridge club meets weekly.
These domestic matrons of the fifties,
bound together in servitude,
in the search for perfection,
wait patiently for the game to begin.

Their homes a citadel of soap
and wax, the reassuring smell
of pot roast on Sunday. Their lives
a testimony to ambition
held captive in denial.

The one weekly indulgence-
to gather with finger sandwiches
and tea, to rise to the competitive
challenge of clubs, diamonds,
spades and hearts.

January Valentine

By Linda M. Packard

The first bite
cracks the shell
of chocolate
& strawberry
scent
rises
pink
as I taste
the softest interior
it reminds me of
our last kiss
so long ago
your lips
still
linger on my heart

Bainbridge Island Press

My Sister's Tea Kettle

By Rebecca Christensen

As a child,
the train whistle echoing
in the night
across our town and
into our shared bedroom,
my sisters and I dreamt of travel
and the ache
to grow forward quickly into adulthood
so we could move out...
move on.

Now as an adult,
hearing my sister's tea kettle
scream into the night
from across the yard we share,
I am reminded
of that time,
that pull,
that yearning.
But now it's for a return to those simpler times
to think back and wonder
at the journey it took to arrive.

Mom's CorningWare® Bowls

By Linda M. Packard

This evening my friend brings diminutive bowls
filled with grapes to set in front of each of us gathered here
to celebrate our collective birthdays.

These white bowls with a narrow bluish-gray stripe
belonged to my mother. This friend rescued them from
a yard sale held to clear my mother's mobile home.

The difficulties sorting mom's hoarded
possessions without her help went on for months.
When mom was settled in her brand new apartment

she wanted nothing to do with her previous life.
I'd take her to Kenmore to find out what she
wanted to keep and what she didn't. As soon

as she entered, she wandered around uneasily.
Immediately wanted to go shopping or eat out or
ready to be anywhere but where she was.

Tonight, I hold the almost translucent bowl
in the palm of my hand; it is small
enough to have held her inattention.

Bainbridge Island Press

The Cherry Pie Story

By Judy Duncan

My scarlet footprints
stain your white carpet.

I am sad about the pie
it was possibly excellent
served a la mode, though
my tongue did not taste
a single bite.

It sat on a high shelf
far out of reach.
Such a delicious scent.
Standing on a chair
I stretched scant.

Being barefoot I was
overcome with passion
to feel warm round
cherries
between my toes.

A New Shade of Lipstick

By Barb Clark

My friend had her lips tattooed,
saying it was something she'd wanted to do
for a long time and I said, brilliant.
If there's ever a place to get tattooed,
it's on the lips.
And she said, that way there's no need for lipstick
ever again, even if it means the same color
every day--no mocha passion or raspberry sorbet,
just tattoo plum or whatever it is.

At our age skin has started to hang, oh so slightly
from the bones, and lips tattooed anywhere else
might start to droop, a slow sag tugging
the corner of a perky smile downward;
no tattooed lips with tongue just so, lascivious in
its juiciness and peeking out
from the upper edge of cleavage;
nor a tattooed triceps mouth making
the perfect print of a lipstick kiss.
No, her lips smack, impeccably saucy,
matching the twinkle in her eye.

Bainbridge Island Press

Hidden Uncle

By Scot Hedrick

You were sketched by whispers
And kept hidden in a distant branch
Of our family tree.

Who were you in life?
Was wine rejection's palliative?
Did forbidden love drive you away?

In another time and place
Could you have been my mentor,
Showing me the tricks of navigation?

Truth was buried deep in silence,
Although time has eroded
Some of mendacity's soil.

I can now add some detail to the sketch,
But a true portrait is denied me,
And left me with sad speculation.

Head Count

By Diane Moser

year after year
they drop like
overripe plums

those we chose
those that chose us
friends that rode our decade

comrades in school
buddies at work
neighbors on our block

pillars that held us up
now fallen
now shadowed pictures

in a faded album
they tiptoed away
before we knew

they were gone

Bainbridge Island Press

Remembrance

By Carl Jensen

I have carried wine
and a cask of oil
sloshing inside hollow centers,
the wine was dry
the oil filtered.

Now, I think on tears I carry
as in a slim pouch I rarely open
tears both bright and dark
and like rain
sacred.

After Your Death

By Marsha Cutting

Only now,
after your death,
can I see you fully--
or at least as fully
as humanly possible.

At the service,
I collected mosaic bits
of mourners' memories,
facets of you
I had never seen.

I loved the you I knew
as fully as I've ever
loved anyone.

Could I have loved you better
if I'd been able
to see more of you?

Bainbridge Island Press

Replenishment

By Marcia Claire Millican

When my breath is uneven and my body stiff,
I migrate to the woods for a mental and physical lift.

I soak in the scent of cedar and the moisture of moss,
no longer am I hearing the voice of a boss.

I listen to nature's chirps and chatter,
all of my daily struggles no longer matter.

I wander about the stumps and leaves,
realizing the goal is not always to appease.

I emerge with new strength and resolve,
with faith again that conflicts will dissolve.

Mesa Night

By Lisa Ashley

Like the hairline crack of a lover's locket
the moon reveals the merest slip of herself,
white scythe apparition over the land.

The sky darkens above the horizon's smolder.
Stars begin erasing the day's sonic waves.
The moon nestles into sparkling points.
She's hard to find among the river of stars
going about their business of casting light
billions of years in the past.

Here on the high mesa Ancient Pueblo people
tended beans, corn, squash,
hoisted the harvest down the cliff face
in baskets on their backs for a hundred years.
One day they went south, abandoned their homes.
I underestimate the Mancos River,
its consequence, its clarity to its bed of stones.
Its flow attunes to each season like bloom to bud,
murmuration to flock.

Crickets lullaby the sagebrush,
sweet and faint under the star dome.
Small creatures move across the window's glow,
moths, or tiny bats, utterly self-involved,
utterly essential, they fly fast
in this vast, black sacred wildness.

Bainbridge Island Press

Artemis Fishing

By Janet McLain Smith

She's of the river valleys, Chehalis
and Tucannon. Her feet planted deep
in dark earth, she knows the meat and bones
of life's compost. Off the riverbank,
from the river rock, she casts her line long
and again to break without sound
the surface of shadowed pockets. Water,
still moving, is slowed by debris. Her eye
measures the slant of the sun, then joins
the still ones to wait.

She's learned patience by the hour
for years in quiet air. She's learned to sense
the subtle tug of life seeking life,
where a lure can be more powerful
than the ancient call to return. Sometimes,
the taking of her thigh-high waders
up the river bank and home without
the rainbow-scaled and fin-footed hanging
by her side, is what she calls good.

"Artemis Fishing" was previously published in About Place Journal

No Ruby Slippers

By Eric Johnson

"I want to go home", she said
To no one there as she stood watching
The waves batter the coast

There is no more story to tell

Bainbridge Island Press

Bainbridge Island Press

Bainbridge Island Press